Introduction

Fear of poverty is the preoccupation of many people, from businessmen, even craftsmen, it is the greatest fear in every person's life that a time comes to him that he cannot find his needs, and the fight against poverty has had revolutions throughout the ages, chiefly the French Revolution, which he pointed out Many people have boasted it as the bread revolution, and upon reading about it you will find an uprising of hunger and disease, and these are the economic revolutions, based on our curriculum.

And because development and poverty are associated with a purely inverse relationship, the higher the economic development, the less poverty and deprivation. (Baqir, 1996, p. 1)

Any progress in reducing the number of the poor does not go in a high manner, because the battle of poverty does not end, but is getting more difficult day after day, and with the neglect of most poor countries, poverty has become entrenched in the world, showing its might and power in eliminating many people, or turning them into creatures. Grapple with the gel to stay

(http://iresearch.worldbank.org/PovcalNet)

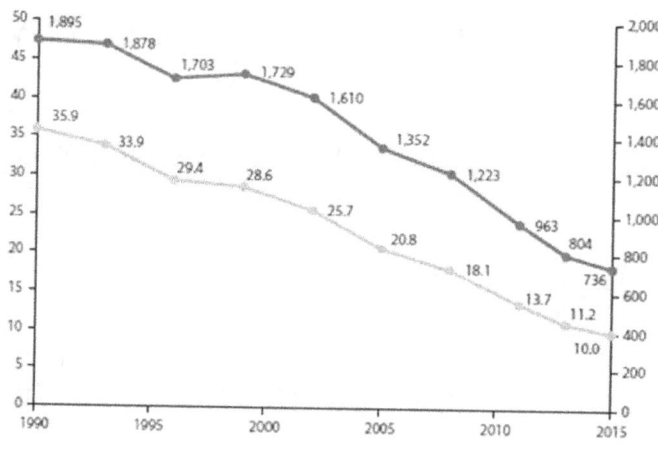

Figure (1) shows the global poverty rate and the number of the poor the reasons:

Poverty causes dangerous repercussions on human life, because: (Farah Bashir Khalifa Al-Amrani, 2006, p.84)

Poverty is the primary consumer of the environment, and an impediment to health care access.

• It causes a decrease in age and the emergence of slums, the spread of crime and violence, and the spread of diseases.

And those reasons are the sticking roots in achieving economic development. Environmental crises generate poverty, poverty supports environmental degradation, from education and low incomes, and the state becomes unable to serve society. Therefore, the high level of poverty depends on economic decline. Income.

(Donato Romano, 2003, p.71)

(Solving the Poverty Dilemma, 2018)

Negatives:

- Poverty around the world is on the increase, according to World Bank sources, as the number of hungry people in science has reached about 700 million people.

Sundberg, 2006)

- Poverty is no longer the preserve of foreign countries only, but it has escalated into developed countries, according to statistics in 1998 (https://data.albankaldawli.org/indicator/SI.POV.NAHC)

- One of the most difficult obstacles hindering the development movement in the Arab world is that illiteracy is linked to poverty, and despite the efforts in the Arab world, we live in a rampant negativity, and the illiteracy rate varies in the Arab world as it drops to less than 20% in each of the Gulf countries. And Lebanon, while it rises to more than 60% in Somalia, Sudan, and Mauritania. (The Arab Economic Report, 2006, p. 26)

Positives:

- Innovation and innovation in the development programs, and the economic expansion of the state, helps it support the lesser groups and provide assistance for a better life.

(http://www.islamonline.net/Arabic/contemporary/Economy/2001/article2.shtml)

- Savings and investment within the theory of development, help to provide productivity that helps reduce the poverty rate. (Lucas, 1972, p: 103)

- Poverty in the Arab world in general is easy to overcome, but it is difficult to apply it in terms of adhering to Islamic law, and stopping conflicts and power struggles. All of these factors are easy to raise the standard of living of the Arab citizen, but what is the point if it does not apply according to methodological principles It is based on the fact that Islamic law is the wise constitution.

suggested solutions:

- Contributing to providing job opportunities for women to help them produce, and providing for their material needs.

Corruption and the duality of money and power

Man, in the midst of his struggle with his chronic inferiority complex in himself, and his steadfast steps in the formation of his growing (I), did not leave a path except to follow it in order to reach a satisfactory state of strength and empowerment, sufficient for him to forget the fact that he was created weak.

It is not clearer than that eternal image (in man's endeavor for strength, perfection and eternity) that of the politician gasping for money, and the businessman who dreams of power, both of which are directed towards the other, and as soon as the emirate and trade meet until corruption becomes a guest at home.

The businessman has shaped himself and his creed is rooted in the love, perpetuation and development of wealth to an infinite extent, and he realizes that one of the paths of wealth is power, on the one hand it protects his investments, and on the other hand it may give him preference (by virtue of the quality of information that he acquires and the amount of power he possesses) over it. Expanding his business and projects, and his hand in power will protect him from any legislation or decision that might harm his business and trade.

On the other hand, the man of power and politics realizes that as soon as he leaves his official position, he may lose most of his ability to influence, and he needs money to maintain his prestige, his presence, the size of his previous relations and his privileges.

Here interests meet, and there is an incestuous marriage that pays the people's dowry, especially in the absence of transparency, freedom, accountability, and general popular empowerment. The contract concluded between the two parties stipulates that the man of authority shall facilitate business, investment and trafficking for the man of money, formulate laws and legislations in a way that serves the interests and priorities of the bourgeoisie, and provide a protection cover for any attacks or excesses committed by the man of money, even at the expense of society and the state.

On the other hand, the businessman fills the pockets of politicians with black money, buys the receivables of the authority's employees, directs the media towards what the interest dictates, and supports the man of power whenever he leaves his official position, either by direct appointment to him in a company or by supporting him financially in his election campaigns in order to become an agent and representative of the interests of a man Businesses in Parliament or any other location that might enable them to influence.

This materialistic, highly pragmatic and Machiavellian model is not born today, it is the product of the accumulation of long and deep experiences from the success stories of the alliance between money and power, that alliance that creates the ideal environment for state corruption and the creation of mafias that guide every decision and legislation, and the state then turns to take care of the narrow interests of the class of money and power over Account of its primary function of public service and the well-being of society as a whole.

Whenever trade mixes with the emirate, corruption and tyranny grows, and the public interest becomes the top priority of the state, while power is concentrated in the hands of a few influential people and merchants of debt, businessmen and politicians.

Someone might say on the other end that a successful businessman is an entry point to the success of public administration, especially by virtue of his experience and knowledge of management assets and efficiency, maximizing returns, and rationalizing waste and costs! This is theoretically Saleem's statement, but what is the guarantee that all these capabilities will not be used for personal benefit and for private companies and stakeholders? Because the suspicion of duplication and overlapping interest is strongly present here, especially in the absence of governance, accountability and transparency frameworks, codes of ethics, disclosure, public censorship, freedom of the press and the right to access information.

As for the politician, it is better for him to continue his work as a committed statesman, not to be drawn into work contracts with tempting zeros, or to a marginal advisory job just to benefit from his relationships and influence the decision, and it is not appropriate for him and his (supposed moral) level to accept working for a fee as an agent for the interests of companies in the power structure.

Politics and economics are two sides of the same currency, but they are not a job for the same person, and the experiences of nations have proven that the combination of commerce and the emirate is a corruption of the public good and a cause for corruption and a loss of the values of truth and justice in the face of material values and short-sightedness. (Al-Banna.2017)

The rich and the poor

Before 1800, nearly everyone was poor. Monarchies prevailed, and there were large landowners, but they were a very small minority, and almost everyone else lived in poverty and destitution. Every human being lived was closely connected to his land. This was the history of the whole of humanity. Then there were some huge changes, and we mean here of course: the emergence of agriculture. What happened is that before planting, people often hunted animals and gathered fruits and vegetables to eat. Then, when the farming activity began, the farmers brought food products to the people, not that the people wanted to bring them. People no longer went out in search of food, there were places they knew would provide an uninterrupted supply of food.

But wealth was tied to the land, and those who controlled the land controlled much of the world's wealth. It was difficult to ship or transport anything. Whether from things, ideas, or people. It was extremely difficult to transport anything, so the trade was not popular.

Thus, the cost of transporting things really mattered, and affected the way societies were formed.

In the seventeenth century, only 3,000 European ships set sail for Asia. And in the eighteenth century, in the next hundred years, about six thousand ships sailed. How hard it was to move anything.

Then, in the years 1800–1820, very important things happened. The two most important developments that concerned most historians were the Industrial Revolution and the discovery of steam power. Then, around 1820, steam power facilitated the transportation of goods and goods, and the transportation of goods fueled industrialization, trade, and economic growth.

But at that time, it was also the beginning – what Dardrey McCluskey, one of the most prominent economists, talked about at the time, with the advent of the Industrial Revolution and steam energy, it was the beginning of what she called the Great Inequality, meaning that certain regions, especially in Europe and the United States, grew richer at a tremendous speed.

It speaks of the emergence of the so-called bourgeois class. The bourgeois were former peasants so close to the royal families that they aspired to live as their own. McCluskey thus considers the rise of the bourgeoisie a very important development because they were the vanguards of the rise of the middle class.

And in the next two centuries from 1820 until now, what happened is that the availability of goods and services increased dramatically. It was not a limited change, but a tremendous change, because before 1820 people were born and died in almost the same world. The world, from the time they were born to the time they died, has not undergone much change. But starting in 1820, the world began to change at a very rapid pace.

Two centuries ago, four out of five American adults worked to grow enough food for their families. Now, one farmer feeds 300 people.

And the reason I'm talking about this is because we have to look at these things from their proper perspective. We have to look at the evolution in the way of human progress – which is what we are working for at the World Bank, development – we have to look at it in terms of what happened.

Chinese President Xi Jinping, as you know, has been talking about achieving great success over thousands of years. And Asia and the Middle East were, rightly, the source of a lot of innovation and creativity before 1800. After that, he says repeatedly, the two hundred years that have passed since 1800 were not as important to China, but

China is now growing at a very rapid pace.

And again, I tell you remember, before 1800, nearly everyone was poor.

At the moment, this is what I see wherever I go: Everywhere I go I see young people who may not have a smartphone, but who have access to smartphones. Many analysts say that by 2025, the whole world will have access to broadband Internet networks.

Now when people have access to broadband networks, and when they can see things on the Internet, two things happen. First, people feel a great deal of satisfaction with their lives when they have access to the Internet. When they get it, they can see how the world works. They can watch movies and TV shows. The degree of their satisfaction with their livelihood increases.

But the other thing that happens is that the reference value of their incomes increases, which is what we're actually studying at the World Bank Group. The higher the income they compare their incomes. And when that happens, your income must also rise, otherwise you will not feel satisfied.

Now technology will do us a great service by making it easier for everyone to access the Internet, but the other thing that technology does is that it will lead to the elimination of some jobs.

There are many different predictions of how many jobs will be lost. Some are content to talk about jobs that will be lost.

Let me tell you what someone has been saying, this person I know well, Jack Ma the founder of the great company on Alibaba. He is the richest man in China. It is a giant company.

" Let me tell you something," says Jack Ma. "When my grandfather was alive, he worked 16 hours a day, 6 days a week, and he felt very busy. As for me, I work eight hours a day, five days a week and I feel very busy. My children will work three hours a day, three days a week and they will feel very busy".

He says technology will displace every function that relies on muscle strength. And he goes further and says that every knowledge-based job will also disappear, maybe not at the same speed, but it will disappear. And he predicts that wherever these kinds of ruptures occur – and he sees this as a big rift, the way AI and technology move

– there will be a major rift. And when that happens, he believes that when these things happen, the world will witness enormous difficulties and turmoil for at least 30 years.

Hence, what do we do? How do we respond to these disruptions? How do we respond to this phenomenon in which everyone knows how others live and their ambitions are raised. They want more for themselves, but at the same time technology could lead to the demise of many, many jobs.

Well, if we go back through history to see how we tackle the problem of inequality and how we tackle the problem of poverty, then this guy Andrew Carnegie is a very important person. He wrote in a book called "The Gospel of Wealth" that he says, "A man who dies leaving behind millions of the available wealth that he could manage during his life will go without anyone crying, honoring or mentioning him. A man who dies thus rich will die disgracefully".

In doing so, Carnegie helped another person, John Rockefeller, see his money differently. Thus began to spread charitable works.

The word philanthropy, which means charitable work, entered the English language around the seventeenth century, and it was a translation of the Greek word meaning "human love".

In 1601, the British Parliament passed the Charitable Uses Act, and this was the first time that governments were believed to have cared for the poor in any given region.

Around the same time, Muslim leaders have seized properties to establish major educational centers. Shah Abbas – we are just talking to Baddih about this matter – the ruler of Persia, who suspended a school from his money in the royal mosque in a move that established a pattern for his counterparts.

Thus was this tradition of acts of righteousness and charity. But the important note here is that philanthropy, which was our traditional way of thinking about how to tackle the problem of inequality and poverty, is not valid anymore.

Let us consider another model, the famous one, Albert Schweitzer. And I find myself in trouble whenever I talk about Albert Schweitzer this way because people – for good reason – admire him so much. But Albert Schweitzer was part of a different tradition. It was part of the colonial movement. He was also a missionary. And there was a sense that it was the responsibility of people like Albert Schweitzer to bring civilization to uncivilized peoples. But Albert Schweitzer has also created the image of a brilliant doctor caring for the poor.

And I heard about it first because there was a cardiologist from the hospital where I trained in Boston who had actually visited Albert Schweitzer in the 1950s. When he returned, he wrote a short report saying that he was terrified by the conditions he found in the Albert Schweitzer Hospital. The man was a cardiologist who was particularly interested in heart rhythm disorders. He said that a lot of patients were suffering from these things, and there were things to be done for the patients but that was not happening. It was a short report, but it turned out that there was a British journalist named James Cameron who visited Schweitzer in 1953, and the following is what he wrote about the hospital he found:

"The conditions of this hospital were a shock to me. I was expecting some violations of the sound rules, but not to this point of blatant filth. The doctor had removed all the images of mechanical progress to the point where he appeared in a horrific form. The wards were primitive caves, with no air inside," And dark, beds made of wooden planks, dry cushions, and chickens and dogs spread in their hallways. There is no running water except for rain, or there is no gas, sewage pipes, or electricity, except for the operating room and the gramophone.

Thus, there are many aspirations and cravings to facilitate access to education, and to ensure that our children do not suffer from malnutrition.

Those aspirations are there, and once people get the link on the Internet, the ceiling of those aspirations will continue to rise. How can we deal with this situation?

This is about the essence of our existence as an institution. Founded in 1944, emerging from the ashes of World War II, IBRD was only part of the World Bank Group in its current form. In a genius move, in my opinion, world leaders, especially in the United Kingdom and the United States, said that before the war ends, we must build institutions that can, in terms of achieving stability, because before World War II and during this war, currency wars were raging. Countries may devalue their currencies, or try to do everything in their power to achieve an advantage, and global currencies were in a state of complete disarray. Therefore, countries needed to achieve some stability in the global system.

But the leaders also saw that an organization should be created to rebuild Europe, and that organization was the World Bank. Its original name was the International Bank for Reconstruction and Development, and its goal was to rebuild Europe.

But then, something happened around that time, and it was in 1946 that was announced in an opening speech delivered in Harvard in 1946 by General

George Marshall and called the Marshall Plan. The Marshall Plan dominated the scene in terms of rebuilding Europe, and the World Bank had to find other jobs to do.

The first loan from the World Bank was to France. But since then, the World Bank has undergone transformations, and its focus has increased on addressing poverty.

The founding principles – – Treasury Secretary Henry Morgenthau opened the conference and said that the goal of the World Bank, and the goal of the meetings, is to create a vibrant global economy – or, in his words that I quote, "A vibrant global economy in which the inhabitants of every country can realize their potential in peace and raise their living standards, And to enjoy steadily the fruits of material progress. Because freedom of opportunity is the basis of all other freedoms".

He also believed that "... prosperity has no fixed limits. It is not a finished substance that diminishes by division. On the contrary, the more that other countries enjoy, the more each country gets for itself".

This was a great vision, and I don't think we've gotten far from that, even today.

Incidentally, the other person who helped prepare the conference besides Treasury Secretary Henry Morgenthau was the great man John Maynard Keynes, probably the second most famous economist of all time after Adam Smith, but he was a very important figure. And that conference, which was not easy, led to the establishment of this institution.

So what do we do? Over the past 70 years, countries have contributed to the paid-up capital, and they have given us money, but we do not take this money, and we are content with just distributing it. We've been doing this in part, since 1962, but a total of $ 19 billion has been paid into the capital of the World Bank Group, including both the

International Bank for Reconstruction and Development, as well as the International Finance Corporation (IFC) which is our arm of the private sector. And with those 19 billion dollars we provided nearly a trillion – or more than 900 billion dollars in loans and grants. So what happens is that if you actually set up a bank and provide it with capital, it uses that capital, and they may – and we do anyway – go to the capital markets to request to raise financing. And we were able to do that in the range of 900 billion dollars.

Moreover, we were able to deposit $ 28 billion directly into an account that we allocate to the poorest countries. This program is called the International Development Association (IDA). The Foundation provides grants to the poorest countries. These countries can pay back over 40 years. Obtaining a loan with maturity of up to 40 years at a zero percent interest rate is extremely difficult, but we do it to help countries grow. And this is what we did from time to time.

When I first entered the World Bank, I saw a sign that read: "Our dream is a world without poverty." She wondered why it was a dream? Why don't we turn this into a true goal and purpose, and we did.

After three to four months of discussions, and this is what we do at the World Bank, we are discussing. We argue about data, we argue about political issues, we debate about ideologies – we argue about many different kinds of tools. We came to the conclusion: We want to end extreme poverty, that is, people living on less than $ 1.90 per person per day, by 2030. We have also committed to promoting shared prosperity and reducing inequality. And we decided that there are three ways to get there.

The first, as usual, is that we have always focused on economic growth, but in this case, we focus on comprehensive and sustainable economic growth, which is comprehensive in the sense that it benefits everyone, and sustainable in the sense that it does not harm the planet.

Second, because many crises affect the world every day, in terms of epidemics, climate change, refugees, fragility, conflicts and violence, we wanted to focus on strengthening resilience in the face of all kinds of problems in the world that affect more and more people.

Finally, the third pillar is investing more effectively in people. The three pillars are inclusive and sustainable economic growth, resilience in the face of the various shocks that occur in the world today, and investing more effectively in people.

Now we have had to change, because the world is changing, and the world has changed radically.

In the 1960s, probably 70 percent of all capital flows, of all the money that went to developing countries, came from official development assistance, of which we were a part. In other words, the money that was going to developing countries all came from donor institutions, USAID, institutions like that, and groups like ours. But take a look here, and see how low it has been. Get on your nerves.

Even in 1990, 50% of all capital flowing into developing countries was official development assistance. But starting in 1990 it decreased, and is now less than 10%. So, we were able to advise the countries what to do, and they were listening because we are a big player.

But now all official development assistance does not exceed 9%.

In these circumstances, what do we do? How do we do our part? How can we help the billions and billions of people in the world who are born today or who are young, or who will be looking for jobs, and how do we help them achieve their goals?

The first thing I told you about is resilience and resilience. This is a woman who lives in a refugee community. Too many people now live in situations of fragility. Two billion people in the world live in fragile and conflict-affected areas. By 2030, 46% – nearly half of all people living in extreme poverty will live in fragile and conflict-affected areas. We are multiplying our efforts in fragile and conflict-affected states, but we also know that every year we do work worth $ 60 billion-$ 65 billion. We also realize that this amount is only the tip of the iceberg. We have no way to solve any of these problems – the refugee crisis, epidemics, famine and all of these problems we cannot solve with our capital. We must find ways to mobilize financing from others.

And so, after the ravages of the Ebola epidemic, we created, for example, a tool for insurance against epidemics. We were so upset about why we waited so long for us to deal with this epidemic. We now have, for the first time in history, an insurance tool that will be activated automatically when diseases like Ebola reach a certain stage. If it were, it would have helped disburse funds much more quickly than the pace at which funding was actually channeled into Liberia, Sierra Leone and Guinea during the Ebola crisis.

And what we did was clear and explicit: Instead of allocating sums of money or resorting to donors for funding, we turned to the capital markets and asked: "Does anyone of you care to buy a bond, a three-year bond, but the capital is at risk" – which means that If a pandemic strikes, you lose all of your money – "But we will pay you an annual return of 8%".

Many people were so anxious to get an annual return of 8%, so that the bond issuance exceeded the supply, and we now have 450 million dollars in our accounts ready to be disbursed if there is a pandemic. We had to pay the return, but it's a tiny fraction of the total.

We are now using the same principle, and we are developing a famine insurance tool. Famines happen from time to time, and we are always late in responding to them. We asked, "Why not create an insurance tool that responds immediately so that we can confront famines at an early stage and stop them, in the literal sense of the word, instead of allowing them to get worse and worse"?

We are doing this, and we are trying to mobilize all the funding we can. We are now the largest financiers of climate change activities in the world. And we're committed to this, but again, we just can't do it with our own money. We must mobilize financing from others.

This is really the biggest game. The size of the global economy is about 78 trillion dollars. There are about $ 7 trillion invested in negative interest rate bonds. This means, you put your money in the bank, but instead of the bank giving you interest, you pay them annually to keep your money.

If you give them $ 100, at the end of the year you will have 98 dollars or 99 dollars instead of 100 dollars. The reason people do this is because they are too afraid to take the risk that they are willing to pay those who keep their money for them because at least it's safe.

There is another 10 trillion dollars invested in ultra-low-yielding government bonds. Another 9 trillion dollars is idle in cash. In fact, people take 1,000 euros of banknotes and keep them in their safes.

Now, we feel like that's the kind of money we need in order to be able to give everyone in the world a chance, and why not? They get very little return and we can help them get a higher return while at the same time providing opportunities for everyone, especially in the field of infrastructure.

And the idea – this is the Guinea Stock Exchange. I don't know why I'm showing you this, but it's just a great picture, the Guinea Stock Exchange. The idea now is that instead of seeing ourselves as lenders, seeing ourselves as direct interventions, we see ourselves as facilitators. And the idea we're talking about now to everyone is the idea of maximizing the financing available for development.

How can we mobilize the trillions of dollars that stand by for the benefit of the world's poorest people? We know that the private sector must play a much greater role in development than before, because there are many, many examples of cases that benefit everyone. Let me show you an example:

Queen Alia International Airport, if you've ever seen it, it's a great airport. The Jordanian government came to us and said, "We need to rebuild the airport and we want a loan. And if you give us a loan – if you give the Jordanian government a loan, its employees will manage it".

And we told them, "Maybe there is a better way to do that. Without taking a penny on a loan, without paying a penny in interest on loans, we were able to convince the private sector to fund this completely".

However, the Jordanian government still owns 54% and thus gets 54% of the profits. And without spending a penny at that airport, they've earned more than $ 1 billion in profits from the airport over the past nine years. They were about to go in a completely different direction, but really great experts at the World Bank Group said, "Why not try this other way".

This is a great example of how we can change the way we do business, not only reducing countries 'indebtedness, but also giving it a return. This is the kind of investment that many people now want to make. Millennials are about to inherit $ 5 trillion from their parents from the post–World War II baby boomers. And what I hear every day is, "We don't want to leave this money inactive. We want this money to have an impact on the world".

This phenomenon, called "impact investing", is of critical importance. What people are saying is that it's not just about risk and return – what are the risks of investing and what is the return. Rather, it is risk, return, and impact. And if the impact is significant, we are not averse to taking more risk and getting a lower return.

It's a great idea, but it's relatively small. It's about 200 billion dollars a year now, which is a very small amount when compared to the size of the needs. The requirements for achieving the United Nations Sustainable Development Goals, or the global goals as they are called, amount to about $ 4 trillion annually. All official development assistance amounts to about $ 140 billion, plus an impact investment of another $ 200 billion. However, we are a far cry from the $ 4 trillion needed to meet impact investing needs.

Here is what we did, instead of saying, "Take a lower return," instead of saying "This is a matter of righteousness and charity." We put in place a system in which we go to African countries, and help them in all aspects of setting up a solar energy tender.

And again, without spending any money, just helping them technically – we now have a program called Solar Energy Expansion. And now the project is paying off – the most recent result was 4.7 cents a kilowatt-hour in Senegal. Senegal pays 15 to 20 cents a kilowatt hour of electricity, but thanks to the solar tender, and because we helped them with it, they're now only going to pay 4.7 cents. This is a great victory, and we will now transfer this experience to another place.

And again, we didn't spend any money, rather we helped structure the deal. By structuring the deal, we were able to get solar power at a low price.

But the crisis that worries me most is the human capital crisis. About 400 million people do not have access to basic services. And 100 million people fall into poverty every year due to exorbitant health expenses. Safety nets cover only a third of the world's poor.

You are all covered by safety nets, but a third of the world's poor are denied this coverage. The worst part of this problem, in my opinion, is the exposure of children to being stunted.

The issue of childhood stunting is straightforward, and it is the child's short stature for age by two standard deviations. We now know that all children in the world grow to be 25 cm tall in the first year and 12 cm in the second year. And there is some disparity, but every child in the world if he gets enough nutrition he will grow that much.

The numbers are really amazing. In Ethiopia, 38% of children are stunted, and we know that stunted children do not get a good education, and it is certain that they do not earn a good income when they grow up. In other words, what happens to these stunted children is that their brains are not actually developing.

This is a study by a Harvard university professor from Bangladesh. On the left is a stunted child, on the right is a healthy child, and the neural pathways are different. In other words, stunted children have fewer connections

References

1. Baqer, Muhammad Hussein (1996): Measuring Poverty in ESCWA Countries, New York, United Nations.

2. Farah Bashir Khalifa Al-Omrani (2006): The Mutual Relationship between Sustainable Development and the Environment, Master Thesis submitted to the College of

Management. And Economics / University of Baghdad.

3. Donato Romano (2003): Environmental Economics and Sustainable Development, Ministry of Agriculture and Agrarian Reform, National Policy Center. Agriculture, Food and Agriculture Organization, United Nations.

4. The Consolidated Arab Economic Report (2006): The

General Secretariat of the League of Arab States, The Arab Fund for Economic and Social Development.

5. Solving the Poverty Dilemma (2018): Poverty and Shared Prosperity, The World Bank Group.

6. Sundberg, Mark, Bourguignon, François, Gelb, Alan and Berg, Andy, The Third Annual Global Monitoring Report on the Millennium Development Goals (MDGs):

Strengthening Mutual Accountability – Aid, Trade and Governance, The World Bank and the International Monetary Fund (April 20, 2006(

7. Lucas, Robert, Expectations and the Neutrality of Money, Journal of Economic Theory, 1972.

8. Dr.. Hussain Al-Banna (2017) Corruption and the duality of money and power

9. http://www.islamonline.net/Arabic/contemporary/Economy/2001/article2.shtml

10. https://data.albankaldawli.org/indicator/SI.POV.NAHC

11. http://www.sidf.gov.sa/

12. http://iresearch.worldbank.org/PovcalNet

13. www.worldbank.org

14.

www.ingramcontent.com/pod-product-compliance
Lightning Source LLC
Chambersburg PA
CBHW070252220526
45465CB00004B/1587